S T A R T I N G   P O I N T S

FIRE

Kate Petty

Photography by Chris Fairclough

FRANKLIN WATTS
NEW YORK · LONDON · SYDNEY · TORONTO

Franklin Watts, Inc.
387 Park Avenue South
New York, N.Y. 10016

Library of Congress Cataloging-in-Publication Data

Petty, Kate.
    Fire / Kate Petty.
        p.   cm. — (Starting points)
    Summary: Examines all aspects of fire, including its traditional
uses, significance in various cultures, and effect on everyday life.
    ISBN 0-531-14060-1
    1. Fire—Juvenile literature.   [1. Fire.]   I. Title.
II. Series: Starting points (Franklin Watts, inc.)
QD516.P46   1990   90-31023
541.3′61—dc20   CIP AC

Series design: David Bennett
Model making: Stan Johnson
Picture Research: Sarah Ridley
Typesetting: Lineage, Watford

Additional photographs:
B & C Alexander 10t; Allsport (G Vandystadt) 30; Celtic Picture Agency
(M J Thomas) 11tl, 15t; Mary Evans Picture Library 29; Chris Fairclough
4-5, 6t, 7tr, 7b, 14b; Hutchison Library 10bl, 10br; NASA 8; Natural History
Photographic Agency 6b; Brian Shuel 18 (all), 27b; Solid Fuel Advisory Service
11b; Swiss National Tourist Board 19tl; Tropix (D Charlwood) 19bl; ZEFA 7tl, 9
(all), 14t, 15b, 16t, 19cr, 22-23, 24 (all), 25 (all), 28.

Printed in Belgium

CONTENTS

Look At Fire

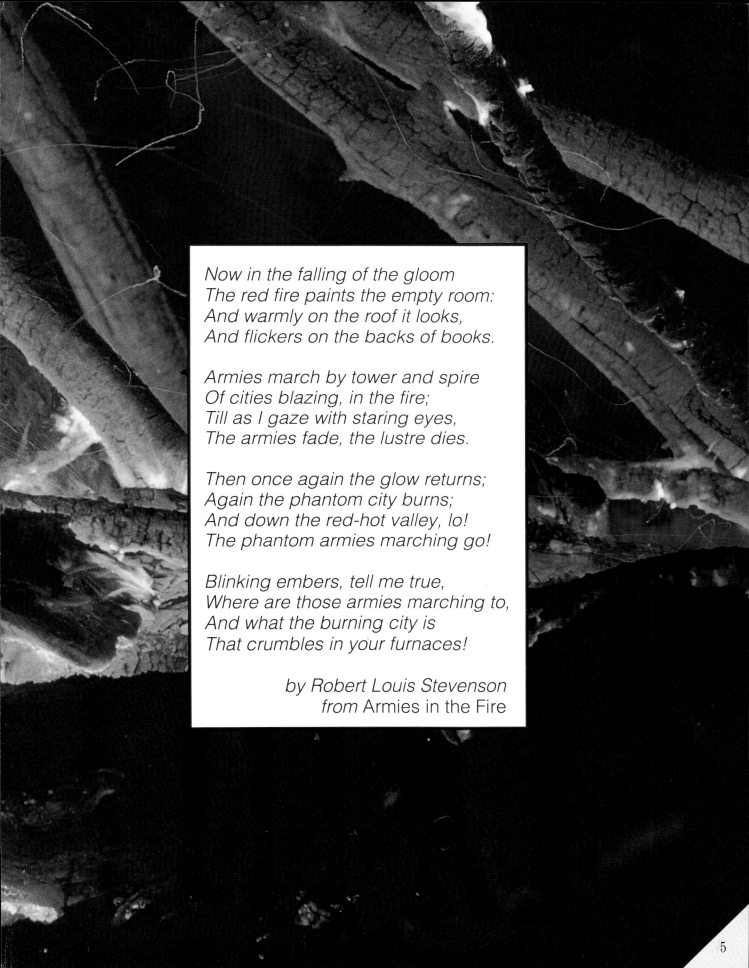

Now in the falling of the gloom
The red fire paints the empty room:
And warmly on the roof it looks,
And flickers on the backs of books.

Armies march by tower and spire
Of cities blazing, in the fire;
Till as I gaze with staring eyes,
The armies fade, the lustre dies.

Then once again the glow returns;
Again the phantom city burns;
And down the red-hot valley, lo!
The phantom armies marching go!

Blinking embers, tell me true,
Where are those armies marching to,
And what the burning city is
That crumbles in your furnaces!

by Robert Louis Stevenson
from Armies in the Fire

From Sparks To Flames

Fires begin with a single spark.

Sparks are produced when one hard surface strikes another.

Fire can be produced in several ways. Early people found that a spark could be produced when a flint stone was struck against a stone containing iron. The spark could set fire to a pile of dried moss or leaves. They also found that a fire could be started by twirling a sharp stick in the hollow of a flat one. Enough wood dust and heat, caused by the friction from the sticks, would be formed to start a fire.

Kung Bushmen of the Kalahari desert in Namibia make fire by rubbing two sticks together.

Making fire became easier when the friction match was invented in 1827. The chemicals in a match head ignite when struck against a rough surface.

The single flame of a candle is a tiny fire that gives out light. In the past, people used candlelight to light their homes.

Campers sit around a campfire at the end of the day. They are drawn together by the warmth and the thought of hot food...

**Fire can be dangerous –
always take care with fire.**

Fire In The Sky

The sun is the giant fire that warms and lights the earth. Our lives depend upon this ball of flaming gases that is a million times bigger than our world and 93 million miles away.

The temperature of the sun's surface is about 11,000°F. It shoots out flames that are millions of miles high.

Our seasons change as the earth spins on its year-long journey around the sun. Countries near the Equator (the middle of the globe) are hot nearly all year around. Countries near the Poles (the top and the bottom of the globe) are cold and icy. But most countries have four seasons – spring, summer, autumn, and winter.

How does the warmth from the sun affect our lives?

The hours of daylight are shorter in winter. There is not enough heat from the sun to melt snow. People keep warm indoors, and animals hibernate in their dens.

As winter turns to spring the sun feels warmer and the days grow longer. Snow melts. The green shoots of new growth appear through the earth.

In summer the grass grows tall and the wheat ripens in the hot sun. Leafy trees almost hide farm buildings. The days are long and bright.

The days become shorter and cooler again in autumn. The leaves of deciduous trees change color and fall to the ground. The low sun casts long shadows.

Hearth And Home

All over the world, families gather around the fire that gives out warmth and cooks the food.

Samits (Lapps) in the far north of Norway keep warm by the fire that burns in the middle of their home.

Tuareg men from the Sahara desert boil coffee in the open. It can be very cold at night in the desert.

Members of the Wasusu tribe in the Amazon jungle gather around a fire in a clearing to cook and eat.

Many houses were built with a kitchen range. It was used for heating the water, cooking the meals, and drying the clothes.

Even in homes with modern stoves and central heating, people still like to sit by a roaring fire.

Outdoor Cooking

Make these vegetable and fruit kebabs, which can be cooked on a barbecue or under the grill.

Vegetable kebabs

You will need:

- **red and green peppers**
- **button mushrooms**
- **cherry tomatoes**
- **zucchini**
- **baby sweet corn**

Cut up the zucchini and peppers. Soak all the vegetables except the tomatoes in a mixture of olive oil and lemon juice (3 tablespoons of each) for two hours. Thread the vegetables onto skewers. Cook them for 6-8 minutes, turning often so that they cook evenly.

Fruit kebabs

You will need:

- **bananas**
- **pears**
- **strawberries**
- **canned pineapple**
- **canned apricot halves**

Cut the pears into chunks and the bananas into thick slices. Soak all the fruit in a mixture of 4 tablespoons of orange juice, 5 tablespoons of juice from the canned fruit, 1 teaspoon of cinnamon, and a little honey.

Thread the fruit onto skewers, brush with melted butter, and sprinkle with brown sugar.

Cook them for 6-8 minutes, turning often.

Fiery Furnaces

Not everything burns when it is put in the fire. Some substances change shape or texture. Others melt, or harden, or even turn into gas. Many manufacturing processes make use of fire.

At a foundry, metal is heated until it becomes liquid. Then it is poured into a mold – or "cast." As the metal cools, it hardens into the shape of the mold.

Potters "fire" soft clay pots in a kiln, which is a large, hot oven. The pots are hard and brittle when they are taken out of the kiln. This is the inside of a kiln.

A blacksmith makes a curved horseshoe from a rod of iron. He heats it until it is red hot and soft. Then he rests it on his anvil and hammers it into shape as it cools.

Glass is made by melting down sand, soda ash, and lime in a furnace. The glass blower takes a blob of molten glass from the furnace on a long tube and blows it into shape.

Charcoal Drawing

You can buy sticks of charcoal to draw with. It makes soft, sooty lines that can be smoothed and smudged into interesting shapes.

Charcoal is made by burning wood in a covered "charcoal pit" where very little air can get to it. Charcoal is a useful fuel that produces a lot of heat.

Create a 3-D effect by holding the charcoal flat against the paper and drawing waves, zig-zags, or fan shapes.

You can rub the lines of your drawing with a finger to give it movement and life.

Charcoal is an ideal medium for drawing large, bold blocks of gray or black for a cityscape with skyscrapers.

Fire Festivals

Fire and flames have played a part in customs and rituals since the earliest times.

Guy Fawkes

English people celebrate Guy Fawkes Night on November 5 with bonfires and fireworks. They burn a "guy" which represents Guy Fawkes, who was executed for trying to blow up the Houses of Parliament in 1605.

New Year's Eve

New Year's Eve is celebrated in many places with bonfires. Traditionally the fire gets rid of the old year and starts the new one afresh. These Northumbrian villagers carry flaming tar barrels on their heads.

Up Helly A

This midwinter festival takes place in Lerwick in the Shetland Isles, Scotland. The people try to bring back the heat and light of the sun with flaming torches which are thrown onto a Viking ship.

Santa Lucia

Santa Lucia, whose name means "light," is remembered in Sweden on December 13, the shortest day. Girls dressed in white carry candles, led by one who has been chosen to wear a crown of candles on her head.

Fire dancing in Papua New Guinea

A masked dancer of the Baining people of Papua New Guinea stamps through a fire during a night dance, defying the forces of nature.

Chinese fire dragon

No Chinese festival is complete without its dragon to parade through the streets. At night the dragon is filled with burning tapers to light the way and ward off evil spirits.

Making Candles

Candles add a festive touch to all sorts of occasions.

You will need:
- **an old saucepan**
- **candle ends or old wax crayons**
- **string**
- **cardboard and scotch tape**
- **molds**

Do not attempt these activities without a grownup to help you.

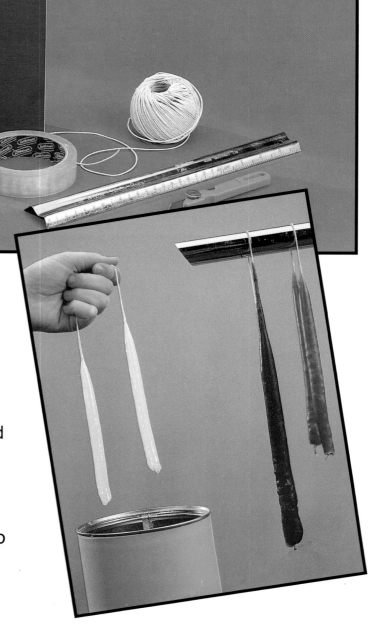

Dipped candles

(You will also need a tall metal container for these.)

Melt the candle ends or crayons in the tall container in a saucepan of boiling water. You can add poster paint for extra color.

When the wax has melted (it should be at least 6 in deep), turn off the heat. Have ready three or four lengths of string 20 in long. Hold a string in the middle and dip both ends into the wax. Hang these up to cool. Keep on dipping and cooling until the candles are thick enough.

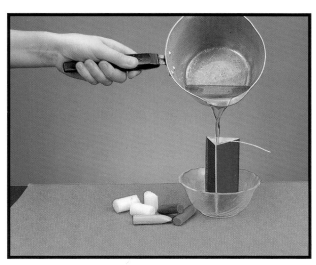

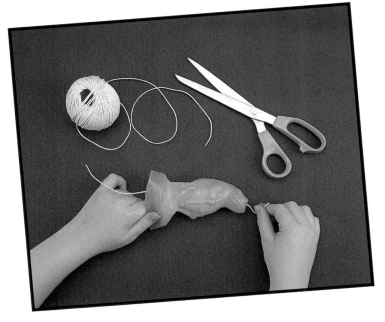

Molded candles

The triangular mold can be made from cardboard, 6 in by 8 in. Use a ruler and craft knife to score down the folds. (Be careful when using a sharp knife.) Join the sides with scotch tape.

String for each wick should be at least ¾ in longer than the mold. Put the string in the mold and fill with melted wax. Support a soft mold upside down over a mug with a cardboard frame.

Remove the mold when the wax cools. The lemon candle should be left in its skin.

Fireworks Display

Fireworks that blaze in the night sky are a part of many celebrations, but they are over all too soon. Cut out and stick shiny paper onto a black background to make a fireworks display that won't disappear.

Use wax crayons for this picture. Fill your paper with different colors. Then color on top of them with a thick layer of black. Scrape patterns through the black with a coin to make another sort of fireworks display burst into life.

Fire! Fire!

Fire gets out of control very quickly. Firefighters rush to the fire as fast as they can.

Most fuels need heat to burn. They also need oxygen in the air. Firefighters use water to take the heat away from a fire. They use sand or foam to smother the flames and stop the air getting to the fire. Some fires can't be put out with water. Oil floats on water, so foam has to be used on an oil fire. Most household fire extinguishers contain foam or a dry powder which can deal with a variety of small fires.

These firefighters are protected by their flameproof suits. The suits are made from asbestos coated with aluminum.

These firefighters tapped a supply of water by attaching their hoses to the nearest hydrant. They can also carry about 2,000 quarts of water in the fire engine, which is called the "pumper."

Bush fires in Australia are often started by the heat of the sun. They spread quickly because the trees are close together.

Forest fires in cooler countries are more likely to be started by a cigarette butt or a broken bottle acting as a magnifying glass. A small plane helps control the fire from the air.

Jack -O'- Lanterns

Make a lantern for Halloween. A pineapple lantern is pretty for a barbecue.

Cut the top off a large rutabaga or turnip and keep it for a lid. Scoop out the middle with an apple-corer or a sharp-edged spoon to leave a shell roughly 1 in thick. This is hard work – it's easier if two of you take turns. Use a craft knife to cut out the features. Always be careful when using sharp knives. Straight lines are simpler than curved ones.

Put a night-light inside your lantern and cut a hole in the lid for a chimney.

In the United States we traditionally make our jack-o'-lanterns for Halloween from pumpkins. You can use a pumpkin to make a beautiful lantern in the autumn, but at other times of the year it is easier to buy turnips and rutabagas. Children from the village of Hinton, Gloucestershire, England, make lanterns from turnips for "Punky Night," a local event which takes place a few days before Halloween.

Always take care with sharp knives.

Volcanoes

Fire from the earth and water from fire.

Nineteen miles below your feet the solid ground becomes a shifting mass of hot, molten rock, called magma. In "hot spots," where the earth's crust is thin or weak, magma bursts through as a volcano. Many of the Hawaiian islands are active volcanoes. This one is Kilauea, sending out a fountain of red-hot magma 1,150 feet into the air.

More than 4,000 million years ago, the newly-formed earth seethed with volcanic eruptions. The gases that belched out from below the earth's surface contained water vapor. The water vapor cooled and fell as torrential rain to form the first rivers and oceans of the world.

Fires in history

Fire at sea was terrifying to sailors in wooden ships. In their battle against the Spanish Armada in 1588, the English sent blazing "fire ships" among the Spanish fleet, setting them on fire.

In 1871, a great fire destroyed downtown Chicago. The blaze began in a barn behind the house of Catherine O'Leary. According to legend, the fire started when Mrs. O'Leary's cow kicked over a lantern.

Find out more about the Chicago Fire, and write a diary account of events as if you were there.

Many places all over the world have their own fire festivals, based on a historical event. Ask your parents and grandparents if they can remember any local traditions to do with fire.

In 1666, a great fire destroyed most of the city of London, England.

Cowboy cooking

Cowboys and campers have always made dough to cook over an open fire. Make dough from two handfuls of self-rising flour, a pinch of salt, and a little water. Make little flat cakes with the dough, ready to fry in a greased frying pan. When the dough is cooked on both sides, it can be eaten with butter and jam.

Cautionary verses

Cautionary verses are funny poems written about the terrible things that can happen to children who misbehave. You can read about "The Dreadful Story of Harriet and the Matches" in *Struwwelpeter* and Hilaire Belloc has written about "Matilda, who told lies and was burned to death." Both these poems have a very serious message, even though they make you laugh. With a group, try and write your own cautionary verse about the dangers of playing with fire.

Did you know?

• A wax candle burns like this: heat from the burning wick turns the wax to liquid. The liquid is drawn up the wick. As it heats up, the liquid wax becomes wax vapor. It is the vapor that burns and makes the flame.

• Glowing particles of carbon are what make a flame yellow. Some carbon becomes the gas carbon dioxide. The rest is soot.

• Heat and sparks are often caused by "friction" – rubbing. If you rub your hands together very fast, they will become hot.

• At the start of the Olympic Games the Olympic torch is carried by a series of athletes from Greece to the Olympic stadium on foot, by ship and by plane. The torch is a "Milner's lamp," which burns kerosene.

A fire quiz

1. How hot is the surface of the sun?
a) 212 °F
b) 11,000 °F
c) 1,832 °F

2. Who uses a kiln?
a) a potter
b) a glass blower
c) a blacksmith

3. What two things are necessary to keep fuel burning?
a) air
b) heat
c) matches
d) sunshine
e) water
f) ashes

4. What happens when you heat water over a fire for a long time?
a) no change
b) it turns into ice
c) it turns into steam

5. Which of these liquids might catch fire?
a) milk
b) paint
c) gasoline
d) brandy
e) water
f) coffee

6. How far below the earth's surface would you find hot, molten rock?
a) 6 feet
b) 3 miles
c) 19 miles

Fire words

What do you see when you stare into the embers of a fire? These words will help you to write a poem or a story.

ash	heat	blaze	lick	amber	hissing
charcoal	inferno	burn	raze	bronze	hot
cinders	kindling	burnish	scald	burned out	magenta
combustion	log	crackle	scorch	charred	roaring
ember	smoke	flare	shine	copper	rosy
flame	soot	flash	singe	crimson	scarlet
flint	spark	flicker	sizzle	dazzling	shadowy
gas	tinder	glaze	sparkle	fiery	vermilion
glare	torch	gleam	spurt	flaming	
grate	twilight	glint		fluorescent	
hearth		glow		golden	

Index

Fire quiz answers

1. b).
2. a).
3. a) and b).
4. c).
5. b), c) and d).
6. c).